BOSS UP

The Surprising Benefits of Working for Your Boss and How It Can Propel Your Success.

Christian Riley

CONTENTS

INTRODUCTION

We spend a significant portion of our lives at work, and our relationships with our bosses can play a crucial role in our success and overall job satisfaction. However, we often hear about how challenging bosses can be, and how toxic work environments can have a detrimental effect on our well-being. As a result, we may be quick to dismiss the idea that working for your boss can have any positive impact on our careers.

In "Boss Up: The Surprising Benefits of Working for Your Boss and How It Can Propel Your Success," we'll explore the importance of working for a boss and why it matters, debunking common myths about bosses, and building a strong boss-employee relationship. We'll also dive into the benefits of working for a good, challenging, or difficult boss, and why your boss should be your mentor. Learning from failure is a crucial part of success, and we'll discuss how working for a boss can help you learn from failure and build confidence. We'll also explore the value of networking and skill development, as well as the role of confidence in achieving success.

If you're considering starting your own business, we'll explain the benefits of having prior work experience before becoming an entrepreneur. Throughout this book, we encourage you to embrace the opportunity to work for your boss and maximize your potential for success.

So, let's get started on our journey to Boss Up and discover how working for your boss can propel your success!

PREFACE

As a society, we often focus on the negative aspects of working for our bosses, from toxic work environments to micromanagement and power struggles. These negative narratives can leave us feeling disempowered and discouraged, leading us to believe that we have little control over our career paths.

However, our experiences working with bosses have taught us that there is another side to the story. We've seen firsthand how building a strong relationship with your boss can lead to new opportunities, personal growth, and career advancement. We've also witnessed the positive impact of working for a challenging boss and the opportunities for personal development that come with it.

Through "Boss Up: The Surprising Benefits of Working for Your Boss and How It Can Propel Your Success," we aim to challenge the negative stereotypes surrounding bosses and show you how to leverage your boss employee relationship to achieve your career goals.

This book draws on our personal experiences and extensive research to provide you with practical strategies for building a strong relationship with your boss and navigating common workplace challenges. We also share our insights into the benefits of working for both good and challenging bosses, and provide guidance on how to deal with difficult bosses and maintain a positive attitude in the face of adversity.

We hope that by reading this book, you'll gain a new perspective on your work relationships and be inspired to take ownership of your career development. Whether you're just starting out or looking to take your career to the next level, "Boss Up" will provide you with the tools you need to thrive in the workplace and achieve your goals.

So, let's dive in and discover the surprising benefits of working for your boss!

BOSS UP

The Surprising Benefits of Working for Your Boss and How It Can Propel Your Success

CHAPTER 1

WHY WORKING FOR
YOUR BOSS MATTERS

In today's competitive job market, it's easy to fall into the trap of thinking that your boss is just someone who signs your paycheck and assigns your tasks. But the truth is, your boss can play a much more important role in your career than you might realize.

In this chapter, we'll explore the surprising benefits of working for your boss and how it can propel your success.

First and foremost, your boss is your primary connection to the company and its leadership. They have the inside scoop on what's happening behind the scenes, from the company's strategy to its goals and priorities. By building a strong relationship with your boss, you can gain valuable insight into the company's direction and position yourself as a trusted and knowledgeable team member.

But it's not just about the company's big picture. Your boss also plays a crucial role in your day-to-day work life. They're the ones who assign you tasks, provide feedback, and evaluate your performance. By working closely with your boss, you can gain a better understanding of what's expected of you and how you can excel in your role.

Moreover, a good boss can be a mentor and advocate for your career growth. They can provide guidance and feedback on your career goals, help you identify opportunities for advancement, and even connect you with other professionals in your field. By actively seeking out your boss's guidance and support, you can accelerate your professional development and take your career to the next level.

But what if you don't have a great relationship with your boss? It's true that not all bosses are created equal, and some can be difficult to work with. But even in these situations, there are still benefits to be gained from working for your boss. By taking the initiative to build a stronger relationship, you can learn valuable skills like conflict resolution, communication, and adaptability. You can also demonstrate your professionalism and commitment to your job, which can pay off in the long run.

In short, working for your boss matters more than you might think. By cultivating a strong relationship with your boss, you can gain valuable insights into the company, excel in your role, and accelerate your career growth. Even in difficult situations, there are still opportunities to learn and grow. So don't underestimate the power of your boss - embrace it, and watch your career soar.

The Importance of Working for a Boss

In today's competitive job market, working for a boss may not seem like the most glamorous or exciting prospect. However, having a boss is an essential part of the modern workplace, and working for one can be a valuable experience that can help you grow both personally and professionally. we'll explore the importance of working for a boss and what you can gain from the experience.

1. **Access to Mentorship and Guidance**: One of the most significant benefits of working for a boss is the opportunity to receive mentorship and guidance. A

boss who is invested in your success can provide you with advice, feedback, and insights into your work that you may not get from anyone else. They can help you identify your strengths and weaknesses, offer suggestions for improvement, and give you a sense of direction as you navigate your career.

2. **Exposure to Different Perspectives and Approaches**: Working for a boss can also expose you to different perspectives and approaches to work. Everyone has their own unique style, and by working closely with your boss, you can observe how they approach challenges and solve problems. This exposure can be invaluable as you develop your own skills and find your own approach to work.

3. **Opportunities for Professional Development**: Another advantage of working for a boss is the potential for professional development opportunities. Your boss may have access to training programs, conferences, or networking events that can help you build your skills and expand your professional network. They may also be able to offer you stretch assignments or challenging projects that allow you to develop new skills and demonstrate your abilities.

4. **Accountability and Feedback**: A boss can also help keep you accountable and provide feedback on your work. They can set expectations for your performance and help you track your progress over time. They can also provide constructive feedback on your work, helping you identify areas where you can improve and giving you credit for your successes.

5. **Career Advancement Opportunities**: Finally, working for a boss can open up new opportunities for career advancement. A boss who is invested in your success may be able to recommend you for promotions, connect you with other professionals in your field, or even serve as a reference when you're looking for your next job. By

building a strong relationship with your boss, you can position yourself for long-term success in your career.

In conclusion, working for a boss is a valuable experience that can help you grow both personally and professionally. By taking advantage of the mentorship, guidance, and opportunities for development that a boss can provide, you can position yourself for long-term success and advance your career to new heights. So embrace the role of working for a boss, and make the most of the experience.

Debunking the Myths about Bosses

Bosses often get a bad reputation. They're seen as micromanagers, tyrants, or simply people who are out of touch with the day-to-day realities of their employees. However, many of these perceptions are based on myths and misconceptions rather than reality. we'll debunk some of the most common myths about bosses and shed some light on the reality of working for one.

Myth #1: Bosses are out of touch with their employees.

This myth is often perpetuated by the idea that bosses are too busy or too important to take an interest in their employees' lives. However, in reality, many bosses make a conscious effort to get to know their employees and understand their needs and concerns. They may hold regular check-ins or one-on-one meetings to stay informed about their employees' work and career aspirations.

Myth #2: Bosses are always micromanagers.

While there are certainly bosses who fall into the micromanager category, this is far from the norm. Many bosses understand the importance of delegating tasks and giving their employees the autonomy to complete their work in their own way. They may provide guidance and feedback, but they also trust their employees to do their jobs and make decisions on their own.

Myth #3: Bosses are only interested in their own success.

While it's true that bosses have their own goals and objectives, many also understand that their success is closely tied to the success of their team. A boss who is invested in their employees' success will take steps to support them, offer guidance and feedback, and advocate for their advancement within the company.

Myth #4: Bosses are unapproachable and intimidating.

It's easy to see why this myth exists - after all, bosses often hold positions of authority and are responsible for making difficult decisions. However, many bosses understand the importance of being approachable and accessible to their employees. They may hold open-door policies, encourage feedback and input from their team, and make an effort to create a positive and inclusive work environment.

Myth #5: Bosses are only interested in the bottom line.

While bosses are certainly responsible for the financial success of their company, many also understand the importance of employee satisfaction and well-being. A boss who values their employees' happiness and work-life balance may offer flexible schedules, remote work options, or other perks that make the job more enjoyable and fulfilling.

In conclusion, bosses are often misunderstood and unfairly maligned. While there are certainly bad bosses out there, many are invested in their employees' success and well-being. By dispelling these myths and understanding the reality of working for a boss, employees can build stronger relationships with their superiors and work together to achieve their shared goals.

CHAPTER 2

BUILDING A STRONG BOSS-EMPLOYEE RELATIONSHIP

A strong relationship between a boss and employee is essential for a successful and productive work environment. When employees feel valued, respected, and supported, they are more likely to be motivated and engaged in their work. In this chapter, we'll discuss some key strategies for building a strong boss-employee relationship.

1. **Communication**: Effective communication is the foundation of any strong relationship, and the boss-employee relationship is no exception. Bosses should make an effort to communicate clearly and regularly with their employees. This can include holding regular check-ins or one-on-one meetings, providing feedback on work performance, and being available to answer questions or address concerns.

On the other hand, employees should also make an effort to communicate openly and honestly with their boss. This can include asking for feedback, sharing their career aspirations, and raising concerns or issues that may be impacting their work.

2. **Trust**: is another crucial component of a strong boss-employee relationship. Bosses should trust their employees to do their jobs and make decisions on their own, while also providing guidance and support when needed. Employees, in turn, should trust that their boss

has their best interests in mind and is working to support their career growth and success.

3. **Recognition and Feedback**: Recognizing and providing feedback to employees is another important way to build a strong boss-employee relationship. Bosses should make an effort to acknowledge and celebrate their employees' successes, while also providing constructive feedback to help them improve and grow. This can include regular performance reviews, setting goals and objectives, and providing opportunities for professional development and training.

4. **Flexibility**: In today's fast-paced work environment, flexibility is becoming increasingly important. Bosses who are willing to offer flexible work arrangements, such as remote work or flexible schedules, can build stronger relationships with their employees. This shows that they value their employees' work-life balance and are willing to accommodate their needs when possible.

5. **Empathy**: Finally, empathy is a key ingredient in building a strong boss-employee relationship. Bosses who take the time to understand their employees' perspectives, needs, and concerns can create a more positive and supportive work environment. This can include showing compassion when an employee is going through a difficult time, offering support and resources for mental health and wellness, and being open to feedback and suggestions for improving the work environment.

In conclusion, building a strong boss-employee relationship takes time and effort, but it's well worth it. Bosses can create a positive and productive work environment that fosters employee growth and success.

The impact of a positive relationship

on job satisfaction

A positive relationship between a boss and employee can have a significant impact on job satisfaction. When employees feel supported and valued by their boss, they are more likely to be engaged and motivated in their work. This, in turn, can lead to increased job satisfaction and a sense of fulfillment in their career.

A positive boss-employee relationship can also lead to increased loyalty and retention. When employees feel connected to their boss and the company, they are less likely to seek out new job opportunities. This can save the company time and money on recruitment and training costs.

On the other hand, a negative boss-employee relationship can have the opposite effect. Employees who feel unsupported or undervalued by their boss are more likely to be disengaged and unmotivated in their work. This can lead to decreased job satisfaction and increased turnover.

A positive boss-employee relationship can also lead to increased productivity and better overall performance. When employees feel comfortable approaching their boss with questions or concerns, they are more likely to feel confident in their work and produce high-quality results.

Overall, building a positive boss-employee relationship is essential for creating a productive and satisfying work environment. By investing time and effort into communication, trust, recognition and feedback, flexibility, and empathy, bosses can create a supportive and successful workplace culture that benefits both employees and the company.

The role of communication and trust in developing a strong relationship

Communication and trust are two essential ingredients in developing a strong relationship between a boss and employee.

Effective communication is the foundation of any strong relationship, and it is especially important in the boss-employee relationship. Regular and open communication allows both the boss and employee to share their thoughts, ideas, concerns, and expectations with one another. This helps to build a deeper understanding of each other's perspectives and can help to prevent misunderstandings or conflicts from arising.

Communication can take many forms, such as regular check-ins, team meetings, one-on-one meetings, and performance reviews. In each of these situations, both the boss and employee should actively listen to each other and be open to feedback and suggestions for improvement.

Effective communication also involves being transparent and honest with each other, which can help to build trust over time.

Trust is another crucial component in developing a strong boss-employee relationship. When there is a high level of trust between a boss and employee, the employee is more likely to feel comfortable taking risks and making decisions on their own. This can lead to increased autonomy and a sense of empowerment in their work.

Building trust takes time and effort. Bosses can build trust by being consistent and dependable in their actions and decisions, following through on promises, and being transparent in their communication. Employees can build trust by being reliable, honest, and accountable for their work.

In addition to communication and trust, recognition and feedback are also important for developing a strong relationship between a boss and employee. Regularly acknowledging and celebrating successes and providing constructive feedback can help to build a culture of support and growth.

Overall, communication and trust are critical components in developing a strong relationship between a boss and employee. By prioritizing open and honest communication and building a culture of trust and transparency, bosses can create a positive and productive work environment that fosters employee growth and success.

CHAPTER 3

WHY HAVING A BOSS CAN BE BENEFICIAL TO YOU

Working for a boss can provide numerous benefits that can help employees grow professionally and personally.

The benefits of working for a good boss

A good boss can provide numerous benefits for employees that can help propel their success. Here are some of the top benefits of working for a good boss:

1. **Career Growth and Development**: A good boss can help employees grow and develop in their careers. They can provide guidance, mentorship, and opportunities for learning and development. By investing in their employees' growth, good bosses can help them build skills and experience that can lead to promotions or other career advancements.

2. **Increased Job Satisfaction**: Employees who work for a good boss tend to have higher job satisfaction. When employees feel valued, supported, and appreciated by their boss, they are more likely to be engaged and motivated in their work. This can lead to a sense of fulfillment in their career and increased job satisfaction.

3. **Positive Work Environment**: Good bosses can create a positive work environment that fosters collaboration, teamwork, and open communication. This can lead to a more cohesive and productive team, where employees

feel comfortable sharing their ideas and contributing to the company's success.

4. **Better Performance and Productivity**: When employees work for a good boss, they tend to be more productive and perform better. Good bosses provide clear direction and expectations, provide regular feedback, and recognize employees' contributions. This can help to motivate employees to perform at their best and produce high-quality work.

5. **Improved Health and Well-Being**: Working for a good boss can also have a positive impact on employees' health and well-being. A good boss can provide a supportive and flexible work environment that allows employees to balance their work and personal life. This can reduce stress and promote a healthier work-life balance.

6. **Increased Loyalty and Retention**: Good bosses can also help to increase employee loyalty and retention. When employees feel valued and supported by their boss, they are less likely to leave the company. This can save the company time and money on recruitment and training costs.

Overall, working for a good boss can provide numerous benefits that can help propel employees' success in their careers. By prioritizing employee growth and development, creating a positive work environment, and recognizing employees' contributions, good bosses can help their employees thrive and achieve their goals.

The benefits of working for a challenging boss

While working for a good boss can provide numerous benefits, working for a challenging boss can also have its advantages. Here are some of the benefits of working for a challenging boss:

1. **Increased Learning Opportunities**: Challenging bosses tend to push their employees out of their comfort zones and challenge them to take on new and difficult tasks. This can provide employees with valuable learning opportunities that can help them grow and develop their skills.

2. **Improved Problem-Solving Skills**: Challenging bosses often present employees with complex problems that require creative thinking and problem-solving skills. This can help employees to develop these skills and become more effective problem-solvers.

3. **Increased Resilience**: Working for a challenging boss can be tough, but it can also help employees to develop resilience and grit. When employees are pushed to their limits, they learn how to persevere and overcome obstacles, which can help them to succeed in their careers.

4. **Higher Standards**: Challenging bosses often have high expectations for their employees, which can push them to perform at their best. This can help employees to develop a strong work ethic and strive for excellence in their work.

5. **Career Advancement**: When employees work for a challenging boss, they are often exposed to high-level projects and assignments that can help them to stand out and demonstrate their skills. This can lead to career advancement opportunities and help employees to achieve their professional goals.

6. **Increased Confidence**: Overcoming challenges and achieving success under the guidance of a challenging boss can help employees to build confidence in their abilities. This can lead to a sense of empowerment and a belief that they can overcome any obstacle in their career.

While working for a challenging boss can be difficult, it can also provide valuable learning opportunities and help employees to develop important skills and traits that can propel their success. By embracing challenges and working to overcome them, employees can achieve their professional goals and thrive in their careers.

The benefits of working for a difficult boss

Working for a difficult boss can be a challenging experience, but it can also provide some surprising benefits that can help employees to grow and succeed in their careers. Here are some of the benefits of working for a difficult boss:

1. **Improved Communication Skills**: Difficult bosses can be demanding and require employees to communicate more effectively and efficiently. This can help employees to develop stronger communication skills and learn how to navigate difficult conversations.
2. **Greater Self-Awareness**: When working for a difficult boss, employees are often forced to examine their own behavior and work habits to determine how to best respond to their boss's demands. This can lead to greater self-awareness and an understanding of their own strengths and weaknesses.
3. **Increased Resilience**: Difficult bosses can be tough to work for, but they can also help employees to develop resilience and perseverance. Overcoming challenges and succeeding under difficult circumstances can help employees to build their resilience and become more resilient in the face of future challenges.
4. **Opportunities for Personal Growth**: Working for a difficult boss can be a catalyst for personal growth and development. When faced with difficult circumstances, employees are often forced to think creatively and find new ways to solve problems. This can help them to

develop new skills and approaches that they can apply to other areas of their life.

5. **Improved Problem-Solving Skills**: Difficult bosses often present employees with complex problems that require creative thinking and problem-solving skills. This can help employees to develop their problem-solving skills and become more effective at addressing difficult challenges.

6. **Greater Professionalism**: Working for a difficult boss can teach employees how to maintain a professional demeanor even in challenging circumstances. This can help them to build their reputation as a reliable and professional employee, which can lead to future career opportunities.

Overall, while working for a difficult boss can be a challenging experience, it can also provide some surprising benefits that can help employees to grow and succeed in their careers. By staying focused, communicating effectively, and persevering through difficult circumstances, employees can learn valuable skills and develop the resilience needed to achieve their professional goals.

CHAPTER 4

THE POWER OF A MENTOR

One of the most valuable benefits of working for a good boss is the opportunity to learn from them and be mentored. A mentor is an experienced professional who can provide guidance, support, and advice to someone who is less experienced in their field or career.

Mentors can offer insights and perspectives that are based on their own experiences, and can help their mentee to navigate challenges and opportunities. Here are some of the ways that having a mentor can benefit your career:

1. **Access to Knowledge and Experience**: A good mentor can offer insights and perspectives that you might not otherwise have access to. They can provide guidance on how to navigate challenges, avoid common pitfalls, and make the most of opportunities.
2. **Professional Development**: A mentor can help you to identify your strengths and weaknesses and develop a plan for professional development. They can provide feedback on your performance, offer tips for improvement, and help you to set goals and achieve them.

A mentor can help someone to identify their strengths and weaknesses, and develop a plan for professional development.

3. **Networking Opportunities**: A mentor can also help you to expand your professional network by introducing you to other professionals in your field. This can help you to

build relationships with people who can provide career advice, job leads, and other opportunities.

4. **Increased Confidence**: Working with a mentor can help to build your confidence and self-assurance. Having someone in your corner who believes in you and is invested in your success can help you to overcome self-doubt and take risks that can propel your career forward. A mentor can inspire and motivate someone to reach their full potential and can help someone to believe in themselves and their ability to achieve their goals.

5. **Learning from their Mistakes**: A mentor has likely made mistakes in their own career and can offer valuable insights on how to avoid them.

Learning from the mistakes of others can help you to make better decisions and avoid common pitfalls.

6. **Guidance on Career Path**: A mentor can also help you to navigate your career path by offering insights on different opportunities and career paths. They can help you to identify your strengths and passions, and explore different options to find a path that aligns with your goals.

If you have the opportunity to work with a good boss who can also serve as a mentor, seize the opportunity to learn from them and take your career to the next level.

Why your boss should be your mentor

Your boss can be an excellent mentor because they have a unique perspective on your work and can provide valuable insights and guidance on how to navigate your career within the company. Here are some reasons why your boss should be your mentor:

1. **They Know Your Strengths and Weaknesses**: Your boss is in a position to evaluate your performance and provide feedback on your strengths and weaknesses.

This information can help you identify areas where you need to improve and leverage your strengths to advance your career.

2. **They Have Experience in Your Industry**: Your boss likely has experience working in your industry and can provide insights and advice on how to navigate the challenges and opportunities specific to your field.

3. **They Have Influence within the Company**: Your boss can be an advocate for you within the company, providing support and guidance as you navigate your career path. They can also provide access to resources and opportunities that can help you advance.

4. **They Have a Stake in Your Success**: Your boss has a vested interest in your success, as your performance reflects on them as well. They may be more willing to invest time and resources in your development than a mentor outside the company.

5. **They Can Help You Build Relationships**: Your boss likely has a network of contacts within the company and industry that can help you build relationships and expand your professional network.

By cultivating a mentorship relationship with your boss, you can gain valuable insights, guidance, and support as you navigate your career within the company.

CHAPTER 5

LEARNING FROM FAILURE

Failure is an inevitable part of life, and it's something that everyone experiences at some point in their career. Whether it's a project that didn't go as planned, a missed opportunity, or a mistake on the job, failure can be difficult to deal with. However, failure can also be a valuable learning experience that can help you grow and develop as a professional. Here are some ways that you can learn from failure:

1. **Reflect on What Went Wrong**: After experiencing failure, take the time to reflect on what went wrong and why. This can help you identify areas where you need to improve and avoid making the same mistakes in the future.

2. **Seek Feedback**: Ask for feedback from your boss, colleagues, or mentors to gain a better understanding of what you could have done differently. This can help you develop a plan for improvement and gain a different perspective on the situation.

3. **Take Responsibility**: Own up to your mistakes and take responsibility for your actions. This can help you learn from your mistakes and build trust with your colleagues.

4. **Focus on the Positive**: While failure can be difficult, it's important to focus on the positive aspects of the situation. What did you learn? How can you use this experience to grow and develop as a professional?

5. **Develop a Plan for Improvement**: Use what you've

learned from your failure to develop a plan for improvement. This can help you avoid making the same mistakes in the future and become a more effective and successful professional.

Benefits of learning from failure:

A. **Personal Growth**: Learning from failure can help you develop a growth mindset and become more resilient. By embracing failure as a learning experience, you can become more confident and better equipped to handle challenges in the future.

B. **Professional Development**: Learning from failure can help you develop new skills and become a more effective professional. By identifying areas where you need to improve, you can focus on developing new skills and competencies that will help you succeed in your career.

C. **Improved Performance**: By learning from failure and developing a plan for improvement, you can become a more effective and successful professional. You can avoid making the same mistakes in the future and become more efficient and productive in your work.

The benefits of learning from failure include personal growth, professional development, and improved performance, all of which can propel your success in your career.

The role of failure in success

The role of failure in success is often underestimated. Many people believe that success is a result of a perfect track record, but in reality, failure is often a necessary step on the path to success. Here are some reasons why failure can play a crucial role in achieving success:

i. **Failure can teach us valuable lessons**: When we experience failure, we have the opportunity to reflect on what went wrong and learn from our mistakes. These lessons can be applied to future situations, helping us to avoid making the same mistakes again.

ii. **Failure can lead to innovation**: When we fail, we are forced to think outside of the box and come up with new solutions. This creativity can lead to innovation and new ideas that can propel our success.

iii. **Failure can build resilience**: When we experience failure and learn how to overcome it, we become more resilient. This resilience can help us to bounce back from future setbacks and stay motivated towards our goals.

iv. **Failure can provide motivation**: When we fail, we often feel a sense of motivation to try again and succeed. This motivation can fuel our drive towards success and help us to achieve even greater things.

v. **Failure can lead to new opportunities**: Sometimes, failure can open doors to new opportunities that we wouldn't have otherwise considered. By embracing failure as a learning experience, we can be open to these new opportunities and use them to propel our success.

Failure can be a necessary step on the path towards success. It's important to embrace failure as a learning experience and use it to grow and develop as a professional.

How working for a boss can help

you learn from failure

Working for a boss can provide you with a unique opportunity to learn from failure. Here are some ways that working for a boss can help you learn from failure:

1. **Feedback:** A good boss will provide you with feedback on your performance, including what went well and what could have been improved. This feedback can help you to identify areas for improvement and learn from your mistakes.

2. **Guidance**: A boss who is also a mentor can provide guidance and support as you navigate difficult situations. They can share their own experiences with failure and provide insight into how to learn from those experiences.

3. **Support**: A good boss will support you as you work through challenging situations. They can offer advice, resources, and encouragement to help you stay motivated and focused on your goals.

4. **Accountability**: When you work for a boss, you are often held accountable for your performance. This accountability can help you to take ownership of your mistakes and learn from them.

5. **Role modeling**: Your boss can serve as a role model for how to handle failure. By observing how they handle difficult situations, you can learn valuable lessons about resilience, perseverance, and problem-solving.

You can develop resilience and learn how to turn failures into opportunities for growth and development.

CHAPTER 6

THE VALUE OF NETWORKING

Networking is a critical skill for anyone looking to advance their career. It involves building relationships with other professionals in your field, and can lead to new job opportunities, partnerships, and other career benefits. When you work for a boss, you have a unique opportunity to leverage their connections and build your own network. Here are some ways that working for a boss can help you build your network:

1. **Access to Industry Events**: Your boss may be invited to attend industry events, such as conferences or trade shows. By accompanying your boss to these events, you can meet other professionals in your field and begin to build relationships.

2. **Introductions**: Your boss likely has a wide network of contacts that they can introduce you to. These introductions can lead to new job opportunities, mentorship, or other career benefits.

3. **Cross-Departmental Collaboration**: When you work for a boss, you may have opportunities to collaborate with colleagues in other departments or teams. This collaboration can lead to new connections and relationships outside of your immediate work environment.

4. **Professional Development Opportunities**: Your boss may be able to connect you with professional development opportunities, such as training programs or industry certifications. These opportunities can help

you to develop new skills and build your network.

5. **Social Events**: Your boss may host social events, such as team outings or company parties. These events can be a great opportunity to get to know your colleagues in a more casual setting and build relationships outside of work.

In summary, working for a boss can provide you with valuable opportunities to build your network. By leveraging your boss's connections and taking advantage of professional development opportunities, you can begin to build relationships with other professionals in your field.

The importance of networking in success

Networking is a crucial factor in achieving success, especially in today's highly competitive job market. It allows you to connect with professionals in your industry, build relationships, and gain access to new job opportunities, partnerships, and other career benefits. Here are some key reasons why networking is essential for achieving success:

A. **Job Opportunities**: Many job openings are never advertised publicly and are only available through networking. By building relationships with professionals in your field, you can learn about job openings that may not be advertised, giving you a leg up on the competition.

B. **Access to Information**: Networking provides access to information about the latest trends, industry news, and best practices in your field. This information can help you stay up to date on the latest developments and make informed decisions about your career.

C. **Mentorship and Support**: Networking can lead to mentorship and support from more experienced professionals in your industry. These relationships can provide guidance, advice, and support as you navigate your career.

D. **Partnerships**: Networking can also lead to partnerships with other professionals or companies in your industry. These partnerships can lead to new business opportunities, collaborations, and other career benefits.

E. **Personal Branding**: Networking can also help you to establish and promote your personal brand. By building relationships with other professionals, you can showcase your skills, experience, and accomplishments, and position yourself as an expert in your field.

Networking is a critical factor in achieving success. It allows you to build relationships with other professionals, gain access to new job opportunities, stay up to date on industry trends, and receive mentorship and support from more experienced professionals. By actively networking, you can position yourself for success in your career.

CHAPTER 7

SKILL DEVELOPMENT

One of the most significant benefits of working for a boss is the opportunity to develop your skills. Your boss can be an excellent source of knowledge, experience, and guidance, helping you to develop new skills, improve existing ones, and advance your career. Here are some of the ways working for a boss can help you develop your skills:

1. **On-the-Job Training**: One of the best ways to learn new skills is through on-the-job training. Your boss can provide you with hands-on experience, allowing you to practice and develop new skills in real-world situations. This can include everything from learning how to use new software to developing project management skills.

2. **Mentorship**: Your boss can also serve as a mentor, providing guidance and advice as you develop your skills. They can share their own experiences, provide feedback on your work, and help you identify areas for improvement.

3. **Feedback and Performance Evaluations**: Your boss can also provide regular feedback and performance evaluations, helping you to identify your strengths and weaknesses and develop a plan for improvement.

4. **Continuing Education**: Your boss may also provide opportunities for continuing education, such as attending conferences or taking courses. This can help you stay up to date on the latest trends and technologies in your field and continue to develop your skills over

time.

5. **Career Advancement**: Finally, developing your skills can help you advance your career. By building a strong skill set, you can position yourself for promotions, new job opportunities, and other career benefits.

Working for a boss can be an excellent opportunity to develop your skills. By taking advantage of these opportunities, you can position yourself for long-term success in your career.

The value of learning new skills

Learning new skills is essential for personal and professional growth. Here are some reasons why:

A. **Career Advancement**: In today's job market, having a diverse set of skills is essential for career advancement. By developing new skills, you can increase your value to employers and position yourself for new job opportunities.

B. **Increased Productivity**: Learning new skills can also increase your productivity. For example, if you learn a new software program, you may be able to complete tasks more quickly and efficiently.

C. **Confidence**: Developing new skills can also boost your confidence. As you become more proficient in a particular area, you may feel more confident taking on new challenges and responsibilities.

D. **Adaptability**: Learning new skills can also make you more adaptable. In today's rapidly changing job market, being able to adapt to new technologies and trends is essential for long-term career success.

E. **Personal Growth**: Finally, learning new skills can be a fulfilling experience. Whether you are learning a new language, taking up a new hobby, or developing a new professional skill, the process of learning and growing can be a rewarding and enriching experience.

Learning new skills is essential for personal and professional growth. By expanding your skill set, you can increase your value to employers, boost your productivity and confidence, become more adaptable, and experience personal growth and fulfillment.

CHAPTER 8

BUILDING CONFIDENCE

Confidence is a key ingredient for success in both personal and professional life. It is the belief in one's abilities and the assurance that you can achieve your goals. Unfortunately, many people struggle with confidence, and this can hold them back from reaching their full potential. However, there are several strategies that can help you build your confidence, and working for a boss can be a great place to start.

1. **Seek Feedback**: Feedback is a valuable tool for building confidence. Ask your boss for feedback on your work, and use this feedback to improve your skills and performance. This can help you develop a better understanding of your strengths and weaknesses, which can be instrumental in building confidence.

2. **Take on Challenges**: Taking on new challenges is another great way to build confidence. Your boss can help you identify opportunities to take on new projects and responsibilities that will challenge you and help you grow. By successfully completing these challenges, you will build confidence in your abilities and be better prepared to take on future challenges.

3. **Focus on Your Accomplishments**: It is easy to focus on your failures and shortcomings, but it is important to also acknowledge your accomplishments. Keep a record of your successes and review them regularly. Celebrate your achievements, no matter how small they may seem, and use them as a reminder of your abilities and

accomplishments.

4. **Develop a Growth Mindset**: A growth mindset is the belief that your abilities can be developed through hard work and dedication. By developing a growth mindset, you can build confidence in your ability to learn and improve. Your boss can help you develop a growth mindset by providing opportunities for learning and development.

5. **Practice Self-Care**: Taking care of yourself is an important part of building confidence. Make sure you are getting enough sleep, exercise, and nutrition. Take time to do things that you enjoy, and surround yourself with positive and supportive people.

In conclusion, building confidence is essential for success in both personal and professional life. By following these strategies, you can build your confidence and achieve your goals.

The role of confidence in achieving success

Confidence plays a significant role in achieving success in all aspects of life, including the workplace. When we feel confident, we are more likely to take risks, assert ourselves, and pursue new opportunities. On the other hand, lacking confidence can hold us back from reaching our full potential and limit our growth.

In the workplace, confidence can help us take on new challenges, speak up in meetings, and build stronger relationships with our colleagues and superiors. It can also lead to increased productivity, as we are more likely to take ownership of our work and be proactive in seeking out new opportunities.

Building confidence is not always easy, but it is a skill that can be developed and strengthened over time. One way to build confidence is to set achievable goals for ourselves and work towards them consistently. When we achieve these goals, we gain a sense of accomplishment and a boost in confidence.

Another way to build confidence is to practice self-care and prioritize our well-being. When we feel physically and emotionally healthy, we are more likely to feel confident and capable.

Working for a good boss can also help build confidence. A supportive boss who provides constructive feedback and recognizes our strengths can help us feel more confident in our abilities. Additionally, a boss who encourages us to take on new challenges and stretch ourselves can help us develop new skills and abilities, further boosting our confidence.

Overall, building confidence is an important aspect of achieving success in the workplace and in life. It takes time and effort, but with consistent practice and support from others, we can all build the confidence we need to reach our goals and fulfill our potential.

How working for a boss can help you build your confidence

Working for a good boss can help you build your confidence in several ways. Here are some examples:

1. **Recognition of strengths**: A good boss will recognize your strengths and provide feedback that helps you improve in areas where you may need more development. This recognition of your strengths can help build your confidence in your abilities.
2. **Constructive feedback**: A good boss will also provide constructive feedback to help you improve your performance. This feedback can help you learn from mistakes and improve in areas where you may be struggling, leading to increased confidence in your abilities.
3. **Encouragement to take on new challenges**: A good boss will encourage you to take on new challenges and

stretch yourself beyond your comfort zone. This can help you build new skills and abilities, and when you succeed, it can boost your confidence in your abilities to handle new challenges.

4. **Supportive work environment**: A good boss will create a supportive work environment that helps you feel comfortable expressing your ideas and opinions. This can lead to increased confidence in your ability to contribute to the success of the team or organization.

5. **Opportunities for growth**: A good boss will provide opportunities for growth and development, such as training programs or job rotations. These opportunities can help you build new skills and abilities, which can boost your confidence in your potential to take on new roles and responsibilities.

Overall, working for a good boss can provide a supportive environment where you can learn and grow, which can help you build your confidence in your abilities. This increased confidence can lead to increased productivity, better relationships with colleagues and superiors, and greater success in your career.

CHAPTER 9

ENTREPRENEURSHIP AND BOSSING UP

When many people think of entrepreneurship, they imagine starting a business from scratch, taking on all the risk and responsibility themselves. But entrepreneurship can also mean taking a leadership role within an existing organization, and "bossing up" in order to achieve success.

Working for a good boss can provide valuable experience and skills that can be applied to entrepreneurship. Here are some ways that working for a boss can help prepare you for entrepreneurship:

1. **Learning from a successful leader**: Working for a successful boss can provide a valuable opportunity to learn from someone who has already achieved success. You can observe their leadership style, communication skills, and decision-making processes, and apply these lessons to your own entrepreneurial endeavors.

2. **Building a network**: Working for a boss can also provide valuable networking opportunities. You can build relationships with colleagues, clients, and industry professionals, all of whom could potentially become valuable connections for your future entrepreneurial ventures.

3. **Developing skills**: Working for a boss can help you develop important skills that are necessary for entrepreneurship, such as leadership, communication,

problem-solving, and strategic thinking. You can learn how to manage people and resources, how to develop and execute business strategies, and how to navigate challenges and obstacles.

4. **Building confidence**: Working for a boss can also help you build your confidence in your abilities. As you develop new skills and take on new challenges, you'll become more self-assured and better equipped to handle the challenges of entrepreneurship.

5. **Gaining financial stability**: Finally, working for a boss can provide a stable source of income and financial security, which can be important when starting a new business. By building up your savings and minimizing debt, you'll be better positioned to take on the financial risks associated with entrepreneurship.

Of course, entrepreneurship also requires a certain level of risk-taking and initiative that can't necessarily be taught through working for a boss. But by learning from successful leaders, developing important skills, building a network, and gaining confidence and financial stability, you can better position yourself for success as an entrepreneur.

Whether you choose to start your own business or take on a leadership role within an existing organization, the skills and experience gained from working for a good boss can be invaluable in helping you "boss up" and achieve your goals.

The benefits of having prior work experience before starting a business

Starting a business is a dream for many people. However, the path to entrepreneurship can be filled with challenges and uncertainty. One way to increase your chances of success is to have prior work experience before starting your own business. Here are some of the benefits of having work experience before becoming an entrepreneur:

1. **Developing key skills**: When working for a boss, you have the opportunity to develop skills that are essential for running a business, such as leadership, communication, time management, and problem-solving. By working for a boss, you can gain experience in managing people, budgets, and projects, which can be applied to your own business.

2. **Building a network**: Working for a boss also allows you to build a network of contacts, including colleagues, suppliers, and customers. These contacts can be invaluable when you start your own business, as they can provide referrals, advice, and support.

3. **Learning from others' mistakes**: By working for a boss, you can observe their successes and failures, and learn from their mistakes. This can help you avoid making similar mistakes when you start your own business, saving you time, money, and headaches.

4. **Gaining industry knowledge**: Working for a boss also allows you to gain valuable industry knowledge, including market trends, customer preferences, and competitive landscape. This knowledge can be applied to your own business, giving you a competitive edge.

5. **Establishing credibility**: Finally, having prior work experience can help establish your credibility as an entrepreneur. It demonstrates to investors, customers, and partners that you have the skills, knowledge, and experience needed to run a successful business.

In summary, working for a boss before starting your own business can provide you with valuable skills, contacts, knowledge, and credibility, increasing your chances of success.

CONCLUSION

In conclusion, working for a boss can offer numerous benefits that can help you propel your success. Contrary to popular belief, having a boss does not limit your growth or hinder your potential. A good boss can serve as a mentor, provide opportunities for skill development, and help you build confidence. Furthermore, working for a boss can teach you valuable lessons about communication, teamwork, and leadership that are crucial in any career path, including entrepreneurship. Even working for a challenging boss can offer benefits, such as learning resilience and adaptability in the face of adversity.

Working for a boss also provides opportunities for networking and building connections in your industry. These connections can be invaluable in advancing your career and opening up new opportunities. Additionally, having prior work experience before starting a business can give you a solid foundation of knowledge and skills to draw from.

Ultimately, the key to success is not avoiding having a boss, but rather leveraging the experience and opportunities that come with working for one. By bossing up and embracing the benefits of working for a boss, you can propel your success and achieve your goals.

Encouragement to embrace the opportunity to work for your boss and maximize your potential for success.

I want to encourage you to embrace the opportunity to work for your boss and maximize your potential for success. Rather than viewing your boss as a hindrance to your growth, see them as a valuable resource and a potential mentor. Take the initiative to communicate with them, build a strong relationship, and learn from their experience.

Working for a boss can offer a wealth of opportunities for skill development, networking, and building confidence. By seizing these opportunities and taking on new challenges, you can grow both personally and professionally. Even if you encounter difficult bosses or experience failure, use these experiences as learning opportunities to develop resilience and adaptability.

Remember, success is not just about avoiding obstacles, but also about how you handle them. By embracing the benefits of working for a boss and taking on challenges, you can develop the skills and mindset necessary to achieve your goals and reach your full potential.

So, don't be afraid to boss up and take charge of your career. The potential for success is within your reach, and working for a boss can be a valuable step towards achieving it.

Final thoughts and recommendations

In conclusion, working for a boss can offer many surprising benefits that can propel your success. By building a strong relationship with your boss, seeking out mentorship, learning from failure, and developing your skills and confidence, you can grow both personally and professionally.

I recommend taking advantage of every opportunity to learn and grow in your role, whether it's by taking on new projects, seeking out feedback, or networking with colleagues. Take the time to communicate with your boss and seek out their guidance and mentorship. And don't be afraid to take risks and learn from failure, as these experiences can be valuable learning opportunities.

If you are considering starting your own business in the future, I also recommend gaining prior work experience to develop the skills and knowledge necessary for success. Working for a boss can offer a unique perspective and provide valuable insights into what it takes to run a successful business.

In the end, the key to success is embracing every opportunity to learn, grow, and challenge yourself. By embracing the benefits of working for a boss and taking charge of your career, you can achieve your goals and reach your full potential.

ACKNOWLEDGMENT

We would like to express our heartfelt gratitude to all those who contributed to the creation of this book.

Firstly, we would like to thank our families and loved ones for their unwavering support and encouragement throughout this journey. Their patience, understanding, and love have been the foundation upon which we built this book.

We also extend our thanks to the numerous individuals who shared their stories, insights, and experiences with us. Your contributions have added depth and richness to this book and have helped us provide practical advice and guidance for readers.

We are also grateful to the publishers and editors who have worked tirelessly to bring this book to life. Their expertise, dedication, and attention to detail have been invaluable in ensuring that this book is of the highest quality and provides maximum value to our readers.

Finally, we would like to express our appreciation to our readers, whose interest in this topic has inspired us to write this book. We hope that "Boss Up" will provide you with the tools and insights you need to build a strong relationship with your boss and achieve your career goals.

Thank you all for your contributions and support.

ABOUT THE AUTHOR

Christian Riley

I am excited to share with you my journey and experiences through my writing. As an author, my passion is to inspire and motivate others to unlock their potential and achieve their dreams.

I have always believed that every person has a unique purpose and a set of skills and abilities that are waiting to be discovered.

It is my hope that my writing will encourage you to take that first step towards discovering your own strengths and talents, and to use them to make a positive impact in the world.

Through my own experiences, I have learned that life is full of challenges and obstacles. However, it is in those moments of struggle that we have the opportunity to grow and develop the resilience we need to overcome any obstacle.

My writing is grounded in the belief that everyone has the ability to bounce back from adversity and emerge stronger and more determined than ever before. I am committed to sharing the tools and strategies that have helped me to develop my own resilience, and to empower others to do the same. I invite you to join me on this journey towards personal growth and development. Let us together unlock our inner strength and conquer life's challenges!

BOOKS BY THIS AUTHOR

30 Days To A Better You: Daily Practices To Becoming A Better Person

Do you want to improve yourself and become the best version of you? Do you feel stuck and need guidance on how to make positive changes in your life? If so, this book is for you.

"30 Days to a Better You" is a practical guidebook that offers daily practices to help you transform your life in just one month. Each day, you'll be introduced to a new habit or exercise designed to enhance your physical, emotional, and mental well-being.

By following the 30-day plan, you'll develop healthy habits, improve your self-awareness, and cultivate a positive mindset. You'll learn how to set and achieve your goals, overcome limiting beliefs, and build healthy relationships with yourself and others.

Start your journey towards a better you today by picking up "30 Days to a Better You: Daily Practices to Becoming a Better Person" and committing to the 30-day plan. With each passing day, you'll notice positive changes in yourself and your life. Don't wait any longer to become the best version of yourself!

Building Resilience: Unlocking Your Inner Strength To Conquer Life's Challenges

Are you struggling to cope with life's challenges and feeling overwhelmed? Do you find yourself constantly facing setbacks and feeling like you don't have the inner strength to persevere? If so, then "Building Resilience: Unlocking Your Inner Strength to Conquer Life's Challenges" is the book for you!

In this book, you'll discover the power of resilience and learn how to tap into your inner strength to overcome any obstacle. With practical tips and strategies, you'll gain the tools to develop a growth mindset, build emotional intelligence, and cultivate a sense of purpose that will help you bounce back from setbacks and thrive in the face of adversity.

Imagine feeling confident and capable in the face of life's challenges, no matter how difficult they may seem. With the skills and knowledge you'll gain from "Building Resilience," you'll be able to take on any challenge with ease and grace. You'll feel empowered to navigate through tough times and emerge stronger and more resilient than ever before.

Don't let life's challenges hold you back any longer. Start building your resilience today with "Building Resilience: Unlocking Your Inner Strength to Conquer Life's Challenges." Order now and take the first step towards a more resilient and fulfilling life!

Network Like A Pro: Mastering The Art Of Building Meaningful Connections And Boosting Your Career

Do you feel like your professional network could use a boost? Are you struggling to make meaningful connections that can help you advance your career? If so, keep reading...

"Network Like a Pro: Mastering the Art of Building Meaningful Connections and Boosting Your Career" is the ultimate guide to networking like a pro. This book is packed with actionable tips, techniques, and strategies that will help you build a strong network of contacts that can help you achieve your career goals.

You'll learn how to make a great first impression, how to follow up effectively, and how to maintain your network over time. You'll also discover how to use social media, networking events, and other tools to expand your network and build meaningful connections with people who can help you succeed.

This book is not just for people who are just starting out in their careers - it's for anyone who wants to take their networking skills to the next level. Whether you're looking to build a stronger network in your current job, or you're hoping to find a new job or career opportunity, "Network Like a Pro" is the book for you.

This book is perfect for anyone who wants to:
Learn how to network like a pro
Build a strong network of contacts
Boost their career prospects
Expand their professional circle
Connect with influential people in their industry
Make meaningful connections that can help them achieve their goals

Don't miss out on the opportunity to improve your networking skills and take your career to the next level. Order your copy of "Network Like a Pro: Mastering the Art of Building Meaningful Connections and Boosting Your Career" today!

The Art Of Apology: How To Effectively Apologize And Make Amends When You Have Hurt Your Partner.

Have you ever said or done something that hurt your partner, and didn't know how to make things right again? Do you want to learn how to apologize and make amends effectively, without causing further harm?

Look no further than "The Art of Apology". This book is your ultimate guide to mastering the art of apology. With practical tips and real-life examples, you'll learn how to deliver an apology that is sincere, meaningful, and effective.

Imagine feeling confident and empowered to handle conflicts and misunderstandings in your relationship with grace and humility. With "The Art of Apology", you can restore trust, rebuild your connection, and grow stronger as a couple.

Don't let unresolved conflicts and hurt feelings ruin your relationship. Invest in "The Art of Apology" today, and learn the skills you need to make amends and rebuild your connection with your partner.
With this book in hand, you'll be well on your way to a healthier, happier relationship. Grab it now.

BOSS UP